ODYSSEO

The Show

Internationally acclaimed Cavalia pushes the limits of live entertainment with its newest production that is now touring the globe. Odysseo is a theatrical experience, an ode to horse and man, that marries the equestrian arts, awe-inspiring acrobatics and high-tech theatrical effects. Set under a 125-foot tall White Big Top, audiences are transported around the world as more than 60 horses and an international cast play and demonstrate their intimate bond. The stage features a real carousel and a magically appearing 40,000-gallon lake in front of a stunning video backdrop the size of three of the largest cinema screens. Odysseo is a two-hour dream that will move the heart and touch the soul. It is an evening that the audience will never forget.

Le Spectacle

Acclamé partout dans le monde, Cavalia repousse les limites du divertissement avec sa nouvelle production, qui parcourt actuellement le globe. *Odysseo* est une expérience théâtrale, une ode au cheval et à l'homme qui fusionne arts équestres, acrobaties renversantes et effets scéniques de haute technologie. Assis dans le Grand Chapiteau Blanc haut de 38 mètres, les spectateurs seront transportés dans un voyage autour du monde et seront témoins du lien intime qui unit plus de 60 chevaux et les membres d'une troupe internationale. Sur la scène tourne un véritable carrousel et surgit comme par magie un lac d'une capacité de 150 000 litres devant un impressionnant écran vidéo de trois fois la taille des plus grands écrans de cinéma. *Odysseo* est un rêve de deux heures qui touche droit au cœur et fait vibrer l'âme. Une soirée inoubliable pour les spectateurs.

El Espectáculo

Aclamada internacionalmente, Cavalia redefine los límites del entretenimiento en vivo con su más reciente producción, que ahora está de gira por el mundo. *Odysseo* es una experiencia teatral, una oda al caballo y al hombre, que combina artes ecuestres, espectaculares acrobacias y efectos escénicos de alta tecnología. Instalado bajo el Gran Pabellón Blanco de 38 metros de altura, el público será viajará alrededor del mundo mientras más de 60 caballos y un reparto internacional de artistas demuestran su íntima conexión. En el escenario, gira un verdadero carrusel y aparece mágicamente un lago que contiene 150 000 litros de agua frente a un telón de proyección de video del tamaño de tres de las más grandes pantallas de cine. *Odysseo* es un sueño de dos horas que conmoverá el corazón y tocará el alma. Es una noche que el público nunca olvidará.

Troupeau

Les Voyageurs

L'Odyssée

Tempête

Les Anges

The Big Top

Standing 125-feet tall, the White Big Top is a traffic-stopping addition to the skyline of each city Odysseo visits. When spectators enter, they are immediately transported into a lavish and comfortable environment reminiscent of any permanent theatre.

From their seats, the audience becomes part of a truly immersive, three-dimensional experience as a state-of-the-art video screen, the size of three of the largest cinema screens, projects images that transport the audience to a world of dreams. Beginning in a misty, enchanted forest where a herd of horses grazes and frolics under a sky of rolling clouds and a setting sun, Odysseo travels to some of nature's greatest wonders. Without ever leaving their seats the audience is taken to Africa's desert and savanna, the American Southwest, the Northern Lights, an ice cave, verdant fields and Easter Island.

Le Grand Chapiteau

D'une hauteur de 38 mètres, le Grand Chapiteau Blanc se profile nettement dans le paysage de chaque ville où se rend *Odysseo*. Dès qu'ils en franchissent le seuil, les spectateurs sont transportés dans un cadre magnifique digne des plus confortables théâtres permanents.

Ils participeront à une expérience réellement immersive et tridimensionnelle alors que qu'un écran vidéo ultramoderne de trois fois la taille des plus grands écrans de cinéma les entraînera vers un monde onirique. Avec pour toile de fond une forêt enchantée, enveloppée de brume, alors qu'une bande de chevaux paissent et batifolent sous des nuages houleux et un soleil couchant, *Odysseo* voyage vers des contrées où on peut admirer parmi les plus grandes merveilles de la nature. Sans jamais quitter leur siège, les spectateurs verront le désert et la savane africaine, le sud-ouest des États-Unis, les aurores boréales, une caverne glaciale, des champs verdoyants et l'île de Pâques.

El Gran Pabellón

Con sus 38 metros de altura, el Gran Pabellón es en una atracción que llama la atención en cada ciudad que *Odysseo* visita. Al entrar, los visitantes se transportan inmediatamente a un ambiente lujoso y confortable, similar al de cualquier teatro permanente.

Desde sus asientos, los espectadores participarán en una experiencia envolvente y tridimensional que los sumerge en un mundo de sueños, poblado de imágenes proyectadas sobre una pantalla de video de tecnología de punta del tamaño de tres de las más grandes pantallas de cine. A partir de un bosque encantado y brumoso, donde una manada de caballos pasta y retoza bajo un cielo de nubes ondulantes y un sol poniente, *Odysseo* viaja hacia algunas de las más grandes maravillas de la naturaleza. Sin tener que dejar sus asientos, los espectadores verán el desierto y la sabana de África, el suroeste de Estados Unidos, auroras boreales, una cueva de hielo, campos verdes y la Isla de Pascua.

Odysseo is an assembly of acrobats, horseback riders, aerialists, dancers, musicians and singers.

Odysseo fait appel à des acrobates, des cavaliers, des aériens, des danseurs, des musiciens et une chanteuse.

Odysseo reúne acróbatas, jinetes, artistas aéreos, bailarines, músicos y cantantes.

58 000 ft²

The White Big Top spans over 58,000 square feet.

Le Grand Chapiteau Blanc s'étend sur une superficie totale de 5 388 mètres carrés.

El Gran Pabellón Blanco tiene una superficie de más de 5 388 metros cuadrados.

200

The visual world created for Odysseo requires 18 projectors and 200 moving lights.

L'ambiance visuelle est créée à l'aide de 18 projecteurs et de 200 lumières mobiles.

El ambiente visual de *Odysseo* se crea con 18 proyectores y 200 luces móviles.

2000

A seating capacity
of more than 2,000.

Le nombre de sièges est
de plus de 2 000.

El aforo es de más
de 2 000 asientos.

70 t

The technical grid
weighs 70 tons.

La grille technique pèse
à elle seule 70 tonnes.

El entramado técnico
pesa 70 toneladas.

150 000 l

More than 6,000 tons of dirt, sand and stone are used to create the stage.

Plus de 6 000 tonnes de terre, de sable et de gravier sont nécessaires pour former la scène

Unas 6 000 toneladas de tierra, arena y piedra se usan para construir el escenario.

6 000 t

The lake that appears on stage is created using a system of pumps with two behind-the-scenes water tanks. This system sends water into the pool. At the end of a show, the same pumps then drain the pool. To create the lake, 40,000 gallons of water are used and recycled.

Le lac qui apparaît sur scène est créé à l'aide d'un système de pompes. Dans les coulisses se trouvent deux réservoirs d'eau. Ce système apporte l'eau dans le bassin. Ce sont ces mêmes pompes qui évacuent l'eau du bassin à la fin du spectacle. Pour créer le lac, 150 000 litres d'eau sont utilisés et recyclés.

El lago que aparece en el escenario se crea con un sistema de bombas dotado de dos tanques de agua ubicados tras bastidores. Este sistema impulsa el agua hacia el estanque para llenar el lago, luego la vuelve a drenar al final de cada función. Para crear el lago, se utilizan y reciclan 150 000 litros de agua.

10

In each city, the tents are hand washed by a team of 10 climbers.

Dans chaque ville, les tentes sont lavées à la main par une équipe de 10 grimpeurs.

En cada ciudad, un equipo de 10 escaladores se encarga de lavar las carpas a mano.

A 250-ton crane was needed during the first installation.

Lors de la première installation une grue de 250 tonnes a été requise.

Para la primera instalación, se requirió una grúa de 250 toneladas.

250*t*

120

Moving the Odysseo show from city to city requires some 120 vehicles.

Le transport d'*Odysseo* d'une ville à une autre nécessite 120 véhicules.

Odysseo necesita 120 vehículos para mudarse de una ciudad a otra.

Our kitchen prepares 600 meals a day.

Notre cuisine prépare 600 repas par jour.

Nuestra cocina prepara 600 comidas cada día.

17 500ft²

The stage covers over 17,500 square feet.

La scène mesure 1 626 mètres carrés.

El escenario mide más de 1 626 metros cuadrados.

600

DESIGN

Designed by Michele Hamel and the late Georges Lévesque, the costumes for Odysseo's riders dress both the rider and the horse, and were designed specifically for the pair. Some of the most elaborate you can see on stage, these garments of faux fur, linen, leather, cotton and silk of vibrant colors are decorated with various ornaments (gold sequins, turquoise stones and metallic ribbons). They are donned with great care by our performers and make for quite a sight.

Créés par Michèle Hamel et le regretté Georges Lévesque, les costumes des cavaliers d'*Odysseo* habillent à la fois le cavalier et sa monture, et ils sont conçus expressément pour les deux. Quelques-uns des habits les plus élaborés qu'on peut voir sur scène, ceux avec de la fausse fourrure, du lin, du cuir, du coton et de la soie aux couleurs vives, sont enjolivés de divers ornements (paillettes d'or, turquoises et rubans métalliques. Nos artistes les revêtent avec le plus grand soin, et leur effet est saisissant.

Diseñados por Michèle Hamel y el añorado Georges Lévesque, los vestuarios de *Odysseo* visten tanto al jinete como a su caballo y se crearon específicamente para ambos. Estas prendas de piel sintética, lino, cuero, algodón y seda de colores vibrantes, que figuran entre las más elaboradas que se hayan visto en un escenario, están decoradas con adornos diversos (lentejuelas doradas, piedras de turquesa y cintas metálicas). Nuestros artistas portan estos vestuarios con gran esmero, y su efecto es impresionante.

2h

The artists need between 30 minutes and 2 hours to prepare before the show.

Les artistes mettent entre 30 minutes à 2 heures pour se préparer avant le spectacle.

Los artistas necesitan entre 30 minutos y 2 horas para prepararse antes de la función.

365

during a performance. The number of duplicates needed depends on the costume—some require three copies.

Pas moins de 365 costumes sont utilisés durant le spectacle, et certains d'entre eux ont été créés en trois exemplaires.

Se utilizan al menos 365 trajes durante el espectáculo. El número de ejemplares necesarios varía según el vestuario — algunos se crean en tres ejemplares.

The Horses / Les Chevaux / Los Caballos

9

Average age of the horses: 9 years old.

L'âge moyen des chevaux : 9 ans.

En promedio, los caballos tienen 9 años.

9

There are nine shower stalls in the stables to prepare the horses for the show.

Il faut neuf immenses douches pour préparer les chevaux avant le spectacle.

Hay nueve duchas en los establos para preparar los caballos antes del espectáculo.

Cavalia's stables are home to more than sixty horses: fifteen are stallions and the others are geldings. They are originally from Spain, Portugal, France, Netherlands, Germany, Australia, United States and Canada. About forty horses appear in the show regularly, while others are substitutes or are in training.

Les écuries de Cavalia comptent plus de 60 chevaux : 15 sont des étalons, et les autres sont des hongres. Ils sont originaires de l'Espagne, du Portugal, de la France, des Pays-Bas, de l'Allemagne, de l'Australie, des États-Unis et du Canada. Une quarantaine de chevaux apparaissent dans le spectacle régulièrement, tandis que d'autres sont des substituts ou sont en formation.

Las cuadras de Cavalia albergan a más de 60 caballos: 15 son sementales y los otros son castrados. Son originarios de España, Portugal, Francia, los Países Bajos, Alemania, Australia, Canadá y Estados Unidos. Unos 40 caballos aparecen en el espectáculo regularmente, los demás son sustitutos o se encuentran en adiestramiento.

68

At least 68 saddles are used during the show (for trick riding, Cossack riding, dressage, English and Roman riding).

Durant le spectacle, 68 selles sont utilisées (pour la voltige et la voltige cosaque, le dressage, le saut et la poste hongroise).

Durante el espectáculo, se usan 68 sillas de montar (para la jineteada, la dzhigitovka, la doma y la monta al estilo inglés y romano).

We create every show around our horses' personalities. We let them be who they are and we adapt each show based on what they are ready to give us each night.

Chaque spectacle s'articule autour de la personnalité de nos chevaux. Nous les laissons être ce qu'ils sont et, chaque soir, nous nous adaptons en fonction de ce qu'ils sont prêts à nous donner.

Creamos cada función según la personalidad de los caballos. Los dejamos expresarse, cada noche, adaptamos el espectáculo en torno a lo que están dispuestos a brindarnos.

performers are the heart and soul of every . We are committed to nurturing them their comfort and well-being. The Cavalia ased on training methods designed to make es enjoy working with us and performing on rs pay close attention to the horses to ensure quest is respectful and matches what they are r.

quins sont le cœur et l'âme de chaque Cavalia. Nous les entourons de soins et nous r confort et à leur bien-être. L'approche de e sur des méthodes d'entraînement qui visent e les chevaux prennent plaisir à s'entraîner à s'exécuter sur scène. Les entraîneurs sont à chevaux et voient à ce que chaque demande à ce que le cheval est prêt à offrir et le respecte

istas equinos son el corazón y el alma de cada de Cavalia. Los cuidamos con mucho cariño or su comodidad y bienestar. El enfoque de asa en métodos de entrenamiento diseñados ar que los caballos disfruten el adiestramiento y su prestación en el escenario. Los entrenadores cha atención a los caballos para adaptar a cada

15 000

Every year, the horses consume 15,000 bales of hay, 70,400 pounds of grain and 1,750 pounds of carrots.

Les chevaux consomment 15 000 balles de foin, 32 000 kg de moulée et 800 kg de carottes par année.

Cada año, los caballos consumen 15 000 pacas de heno, 32 000 kilos de cereales y 800 kilos de zanahorias.

Our horses are pampe
They are showered, g
tension, and taken on
enjoy the sun.

Nos chevaux sont dor
brossage, massage po
dans les paddocks po

Mimamos a nuestros c
los sentidos: los bañar
masajes para quitar la
para divertirse y toma

Musical instruments: violin, upright bass, drums, bass, guitar, flute, saxophone, djembe, kora, tamtam.

Instruments de musique : violon, contrebasse, batterie, basse, guitare, flûte, saxophone, djembé, kora, tam-tam.

Instrumentos musicales: violín, contrabajo, batería, bajo, guitarra, flauta, saxofón, yembe, kora, tamtam.

All of the music feature – crafted by acclaimed c Michel Cusson – is perfo so that our gifted vocali instrumentalists can ke the horses and ensure t maximum freedom as t frolic on stage.

La totalité de la musique – créée par le réputé cor Michel Cusson – est joue direct, de sorte que les ta instrumentistes et chant suivre le rythme des che s'assurer qu'ils s'amusen en toute liberté sur scèn

Toda la música de Odysse por el aclamado compos Cusson, se ejecuta en vi nuestra talentosa vocali músicos pueden seguir e los caballos y asegurars ellos actúan y se diviert escenario con toda liber

125 permanent employees work on the Odysseo show.

125 employés œuvrent de façon permanente pour Odysseo.

Un total de 125 empleados trabajan de manera pe   anente

CAROUSEL

Text Raôul Duguay, Adaptation Fabrizio Voghera

The universe is an illusion
infinite poetry
Where dreams in a circle
caress the thoughts and the world

The sky like a carousel
If the stars dance
They shine in the silence
Like fireflies

Turn this life turns
still turns without end
us with the nose up to look
Where does the sky go to the end

(Music)

Sailing galaxies with the fear of falling
We linked to this life
with the restlessness change

But until the beautiful moon
will go the rounds the earth
and as long as our earth, then
will be of the sun like a sister

Just a single star
To dream a little bit more in the soul
the universe is here
We turn on ourselves and we never stop
Like angels dancing

(But) Turn this life turns
still turns without end
us with the nose up to look
The great dream shall live and who will
not end, will not end!

Sing the endless love
The color of a star
To stop a moment
The life and his immense circle

Turn this life turns
still spinning endlessly
We us with the nose up to look
The dream shall live and who will not end,
will not end!

Turn this life turns
still spinning endlessly
We us with the nose up to look
The dream will live and
who will not end, will not end!

CAROSELLO

Testo Raôul Duguay - Adattamento testo Fabrizio Voghera

L'universo è un'illusione
infinita poesia
dove i sogni in girotondo
accarezzano i pensieri e il mondo

Il cielo come un carosello
se le stelle danzano
brillano nel silenzio
come lucciole

Gira questa vita gira
ruota ancora senza fine
noi col naso in su a guardare
dove và a finire il cie-lo che và

(Musica)

Navigando le galassie
la paura di cadere
noi legati a questa vita
con la smania di cambiarla

Ma finchè la bella luna
farà il giro della terra
e finchè la nostra terra poi
sarà del sole come una sorella

Basterà una sola stella
per sognare ancora un pò l'universo è qui
nell'anima
noi giriamo su noi stessi e non ci
fermiamo mai
come gli angeli che ballano

Gira questa vita gira
ruota ancora senza fine
noi col naso in su a guardare
il grande sogno che vivrà e non finirà,
non finirà!

Gira questa vita ruota
ruota ancora senza fine
noi col naso in su a guardare
il grande sogno che vivrà e non finirà

Canto l'infinito amore
di una stella il suo colore

The Breeds

Cavalia productions are a symphony of colors and emotions revolving around the beauty and magnificence of our four-legged artists. Nowhere else in the world are horses showcased in such an enchanting, innovative performance setting or treated with such respect, both on and off stage. Odysseo features more than 60 horses from a dozen different breeds.

Les races de chevaux

Évoluant dans une symphonie de couleurs et d'émotions, nos chevaux sont au cœur de la beauté et de la joie des productions de Cavalia. Nulle part au monde, on a mis la race chevaline dans un contexte scénographique aussi enchanteur, aussi innovateur et aussi respectueux, sur scène comme hors scène. *Odysseo* compte plus de 60 chevaux issus d'une douzaine de races différentes.

Razas de caballos

Las producciones de Cavalia son una sinfonía de colores y emociones, en las cuales el tema central es la belleza y la magnificencia de nuestros artistas equinos. En ningún otro lugar del mundo, los caballos se presentan en un entorno tan innovador, fascinante y respetuoso, tanto dentro como fuera del escenario. *Odysseo* cuenta con 66 caballos de una docena de razas distintas.

APPALOOSA / APPALOOSA / APPALOOSA

A breed developed in the 18th century by the Native American Nez Percé tribe, Appaloosas are famous for their colorful, spotted coat and hooves. Adopted as the state horse of Idaho in 1975, the Appaloosa breed was once called "Palouse" because it originated in the Palouse River region.

Cette race a été produite au 18e siècle par la tribu amérindienne Nez Percé. On reconnaît l'Appaloosa à sa robe et à ses sabots tachetés et colorés. Devenu le cheval emblématique de l'État de l'Idaho en 1975, à l'origine, il était appelé « cheval Palouse », du nom de la rivière située dans les États américains de Washington et de l'Idaho, qui coule près du lieu où la race est née.

Raza desarrollada en el siglo XVIII por la tribu de indígenas americanos nez percé, el Appaloosa es famoso por su capa y sus pezuñas coloridas y pecosas. Adoptado en 1975 en Idaho como el caballo del estado, el Appaloosa era llamado antes "caballo Palouse" en honor al río Palouse, que atraviesa la región de origen de la raza.

ARABIAN / ARABE / ÁRABE

Admired for their distinctive, dished facial profile, large eyes, and great intelligence, Arabian horses lived among the desert tribes of the Arabian Peninsula for thousands of years. Bred by the Bedouins as war mounts for an extreme climate, Arabian horses evolved with an unmatched level of energy and stamina. The breed's age-old affinity with humans is legendary: Arabians often shared the tents, food and water of their nomadic owners.

Avec son profil racé distinctif, ses grands yeux et sa vive intelligence, le cheval Arabe vit en compagnie des tribus du désert de la péninsule arabique depuis des milliers d'années. Élevé par les Bédouins comme monture de guerre en climats arides, ce cheval a développé une vigueur et une endurance incomparables. Ses affinités avec l'homme sont bien connues : les chevaux Arabes ont souvent partagé la tente, la nourriture et l'eau de leurs propriétaires nomades.

Admirado por su distintivo perfil elegante, sus ojos grandes y su marcada inteligencia, el caballo Árabe vive entre las tribus del desierto de la península Arábiga desde hace miles de años. Criado por los beduinos como monta de guerra en un clima extremo, el caballo Árabe desarrolló una resistencia y una energía inigualables. La afinidad de esta raza con los humanos es legendaria; los caballos árabes compartían frecuentemente las tiendas, la comida y el agua de sus propietarios nómadas.

FRENCH SADDLE HORSE / CHEVAL DE SELLE FRANÇAIS / SILLA FRANCÉS

Standing at about 15.2 to 16.3 hands tall, the French Saddle Horse is tough and agile known for its strong bones. Like all warmbloods, it is a mix of breeds, but owes much of its genetics to the fast French Trotters. In the 19th century, Normandy breeders imported English Thoroughbreds and half-breed stallions to mix with tough but common all-purpose Norman mares. They produced two types: the fast harness horses that became the French Trotters and the Anglo Norman, the prototype for the Selle Français. They are predominately chestnut colored.

Le cheval de selle français est robuste, agile et doté d'une bonne ossature. Il mesure entre 15,2 et 16,3 mains. Comme tous les chevaux à sang chaud, il est un mélange de races, mais il tient davantage du rapide Trotteur français. Au cours du 19e siècle, les éleveurs normands ont importé des pur-sang anglais et des étalons demi-sang afin de les accoupler avec des juments normandes robustes, mais communes et tout usage. Ils ont produit deux types de chevaux : le cheval d'attelage rapide, qui est devenu le Trotteur français, et l'Anglo-Normand, qui est le prototype du cheval de selle français. Leur robe est principalement celle de la famille des alezans.

El Silla Francés es un caballo robusto, ágil y huesudo, que mide entre 15.2 y 16.3 palmos en la cruz. Como todos los caballos de sangre caliente, es una cruza, pero tiene mucha influencia del rápido Trotón Francés. En el siglo XIX, criadores de Normandía importaron sementales de media y pura sangre de Gran Bretaña para cruzarlos con caballos normandos, muy resistentes y polivalentes, pero corrientes. De estos cruces salieron dos tipos: el Trotón Francés y el caballo Anglo-normando, el cual constituyó el prototipo de lo que hoy se conoce como Silla Francés. Su pelaje es predominantemente alazán.

CANADIAN HORSE / CANADIEN / CABALLO CANADIENSE

The Canadian Horse is a little known national treasure of Canada descending from draft and light riding horses imported to Canada in the late 1600s and was later crossed with British and American breeds. During the 18th century, the Canadian Horse spread thought the northeastern US, where is contributed to the development of several horse breeds. The Canadian Horse typically stands 14 hands high to 16 hands high and is most frequently dark brown, bay or chestnut in colour. Best of all, the Canadian Horse is renowned for its kind, sensible, sociable and good-natured personality.

Le Canadien est un trésor national peu connu descendant de chevaux de trait et de selle importés au Canada à la fin des années 1600 et croisés par la suite avec des races anglaises et américaines. Au cours du 18e siècle, le Canadien s'est répandu au nord-est des États-Unis, où il a contribué au développement de nombreuses autres races. Ce cheval a généralement une hauteur de 14 à 16 mains et une robe brun foncé, baie ou alezane. Mieux encore, le cheval Canadien est reconnu pour son caractère aimable, sensible, social et facile à vivre.

El Caballo canadiense es un tesoro nacional de Canadá poco conocido. Desciende de los caballos de tiro y fáciles de montar que se importaron a Canadá a finales del siglo XVII; luego se le cruzó con razas británicas y americanas. Durante el siglo XVIII, el Caballo canadiense se expandió en todo el noreste de los Estados Unidos, donde contribuyó al desarrollo de varias razas más. En general, este caballo mide entre 14 y 16 palmos de alzada; normalmente, su color es marrón oscuro, alazán o castaño. Lo mejor de todo, el Caballo canadiense es reconocido por su personalidad noble, sensible, sociable y amigable.

FRIESIAN / FRISON / FRISÓN

The Friesian is one of Europe's oldest horse and down the centuries it had an influence on a number of other breeds, notably Oldenburger, Dutch Warmblood, Shire and Holestiner, to name a few. The breed's homeland is Friesland in the Northern Netherlands. The Friesian range from 15 hands high to 16 hands high and is very majestic with its striking black colour, long black mane, wavy tail and feathers on lower legs. Its sweet nature and willingness make it an ideal all-round working horse.

Le Frison est une des races de chevaux les plus anciennes d'Europe qui a eu une influence pendant des siècles sur un grand nombre d'autres races, notamment l'Oldenbourg, l'Hollandais à sang chaud, le Shire et l'Holsteiner, pour ne nommer que celles-là. Sa région d'origine est le Friesland, dans le nord des Pays-Bas. Le Frison mesure entre 15 et 16 mains de hauteur et a une allure majestueuse avec son éclatante robe noire, sa longue crinière, sa queue ondulée et ses fanons au bas de ses pattes. Sa nature douce et sa bonne volonté font de lui un idéal cheval de travail complet.

El Frisón es una de las razas europeas más antiguas; durante siglos ha influenciado un gran número de razas, en particular el Oldenburgo, el Holandés de sangre caliente, el Shire y el Holsteiner, por nombrar algunos. La raza es originaria de Frisia, en el norte de los Países Bajos. Los caballos frisones tienen una alzada de 15 a 16 palmos; su llamativa capa y su larga melena negras, su cola ondulada y el pelo

...las cual tinas de sus patas lo hacen un caballo majestuoso. Gracias a su naturaleza amable y su buena disposición, es un caballo ideal para todo tipo de trabajo.

HANOVERIAN / HANOVRIEN / HANNOVERIANO

The Hanoverian breed was established in Hanover, Germany in 1735 by the King of England, George II. Originally, the horses were a cross with local mares and Spanish, Oriental, and Neapolitan stallions. Several times in its history, Thoroughbreds were brought into the breed to inject courage and stamina. Today, the Hanoverians enjoy a worldwide reputation as successful competition horses in show jumping and dressage. This warmblood is a big, strong, upright horse, 16 to 17 hands tall, with a balanced structure, active and bold character, and brown, chestnut, bay or black coloring.

La race hanovrienne a été établie à Hanovre en Allemagne en 1735 par le roi d'Angleterre, George II. Initialement, ce cheval était un croisement entre des juments locales et des étalons espagnols, orientaux et napolitains. À plusieurs reprises dans son histoire, le pur-sang a été inclus dans la lignée afin d'y apporter plus de courage et d'endurance. Aujourd'hui, le Hanovrien peut se vanter de posséder une réputation mondiale de cheval de compétition performant dans le saut d'obstacles et le dressage. Ce « warmblood » est un cheval imposant, fort et bien droit qui atteint une hauteur de 16 à 17 mains et qui possède une conformation équilibrée, qui est actif et audacieux et qui affiche une robe habituellement brune, alezane, baie ou noire

Fue el rey Jorge II de Gran Bretaña quien estableció la raza hannoveriana en Hannover, Alemania, en 1735. Originalmente, fue un cruce de caballos locales con sementales españoles, orientales y napolitanos. Durante la historia del Hannoveriano, se recurrió en varias ocasiones a caballos Pura Sangre Inglés para dar a la raza más valentía y vigor. Hoy en día, los Hannoverianos tienen una buena reputación en todo el mundo como caballos de competencias de salto y de doma. Este caballo de sangre caliente es fuerte, resistente y vertical, y tiene un carácter activo y atrevido; mide entre 16 y 17 palmos en la cruz. Su constitución es equilibrada, y su pelaje es habitualmente café, castaño, alazán o negro.

HOLSTEINER / HOLSTEINER / HOLSTEIN

The Holsteiner horse is a type of warmblood originally bred in the region of Holstein in Germany. In the 17th and 18th century, Holsteiners were used around Europe as cavalry mounts. By the 19th century, heavy cavalry horses were no longer required for the battlefields so Thoroughbred

and other lighter types of stallions were used to influence the breed. The most noble and sturdy carriage horses resulted, and soon gained significant popularity around Europe. The breed combines the elegance of Thoroughbreds with the dependability, power, ability, heart and stamina of Holsteiners. Holsteiners are nowadays found at the top levels of dressage, combined driving, show hunters, and eventing.

Le Holsteiner (ou Holstein) est un cheval de type sang chaud élevé à l'origine à Holstein, en Allemagne. En Europe, dans les années 1600 et 1700, les Holsteiners servaient de montures aux cavaliers. Au 19e siècle, les chevaux lourds de cavalerie n'étaient plus nécessaires dans les champs de bataille, et la première modification à l'espèce a été réalisée

quand les pur-sang et d'autres étalons plus légers ont été introduits dans la lignée afin de la modifier. Le mélange a créé un cheval d'attelage noble et robuste, surtout populaire en Europe. La race combine l'élégance du pur-sang et la fiabilité, le puissance, l'habileté, le cœur et l'endurance du Holsteiner. De nos jours, les Holsteiners se trouvent aux niveaux les plus élevés dans le dressage, l'attelage, l'épreuve de style à l'obstacle et les concours complets.

El Holstein es un tipo de caballo de sangre caliente originario de la región de Holstein, en Alemania. En los siglos XVII y XVIII, esta raza servía en toda Europa de monta de caballería. En el siglo XIX, ya no se necesitaban caballos de caballería pesados en los campos de batallá, así que se hizo una primera modificación del tipo al usar sementales Purasangre Inglés y de otras ra-

zas más ligeras para influenciar el Holstein. Este cruce dio como resultado un caballo de carruaje más noble y robusto que fue popular sobre todo en Europa. La raza actual tiene tanto la elegancia del Purasangre Inglés como la fiabilidad, la potencia, la habilidad, el corazón y la energía del Holstein. En la actualidad, los caballos Holstein se encuentran en los niveles superiores de las competencias de doma, enganche ecuestre, caza de demostración y concursos completos.

LUSITANO / LUSITANIEN / LUSITANO

Bold, brave, and athletic, the Lusitano is the traditional horse of the Portuguese mounted bullfighters and is revered by the country's classical riding masters. Similar in build to the P.R.E. horses of Spain, the two breeds are thought to have originated from a common source on the Iberian Peninsula thousands

of years ago. Portugal closed its studbooks to Spanish horses in 1960, renaming its breed the Lusitano. Blessed with a thick, luxurious mane and tail, the Lusitano's more convex profile is reminiscent of the old Andalusian or Iberian horses.

Audacieux, brave et athlétique, le Lusitanien est le cheval traditionnel des toreros portugais et est vénéré par les maîtres de l'équitation classique de ce pays. Sa conformation semblable à celle du Pure race espagnole (P.R.E.) semble indiquer que ces deux races sont de la même souche de la péninsule ibérique, qui remonterait à des milliers d'années. En 1960, le Portugal ferme ses registres d'élevage aux chevaux espagnols, rebaptisant la race en Lusitanien. Reconnu pour sa queue et sa crinière abondantes, le Lusitanien a un profil plus convexe que le P.R.E. qui rappelle le chanfrein des vieux Andalous ou des chevaux ibériques.

Atrevido, valiente y atlético, el Lusitano es el caballo tradicional de los rejoneadores y los maestros de la montura clásica de Portugal. Lo veneran por su estructura parecida a la del caballo de Pura Raza Española, de hecho se cree que ambas razas comparten el mismo origen milenario en la península Ibérica. En 1960, Portugal cerró sus libros genealógicos a los caballos españoles y nombró a la raza "Lusitano". Dotado de una melena y una cola espesas y abundantes, el perfil del lusitano, más convexo que el del caballo de Pura Raza Española, recuerda a los viejos caballos andaluz e ibérico.

PAINT HORSE / PAINT HORSE / PAINT HORSE

Known for their colorful coat pattern, compact build, and docile disposition, American Paint Horses are popular the world over. Paint Horses can be a combination of white and virtually any other color in the equine spectrum. While the markings are all sizes and shapes and located anywhere on the body, the coat patterns are just three types: overo, tobiano, and tovero. The Paint Horse is now the second most popular breed in the U.S. breed registry.

Le Paint Horse se distingue par les motifs colorés de sa robe, sa conformation compacte et son caractère docile, qualités qui en font une race très populaire dans le monde entier. Ses couleurs peuvent être une combinaison de blanc et de toute couleur du spectre équin. Alors que les taches peuvent être de formes et de grandeurs différentes et se retrouver partout sur le corps, seulement trois types de robes existent : overo, tobiano et tovero. La race occupe désormais la deuxième place en popularité dans les registres américains.

Conocido por su capa de motivos coloridos, su complexión compacta y su docilidad, el Paint Horse americano es muy popular en todo el mundo. Los caballos de esta raza pueden lucir una combinación de blanco con prácticamente cualquier color del espectro equino, con manchas de cualquier forma o tamaño, localizadas en cualquier lugar de su cuerpo. Sin embargo, sólo tienen tres patrones de pelaje: overo, tobiano y tovero. En el registro de razas de Estados Unidos, el Paint Horse es el segundo más popular.

PERCHERON / PERCHERON / PERCHERÓN

Noted for their substance and style, Percherons are a well-muscled draft breed. Weighing 2,000 pounds or more, their towering presence belies their docility. The breed originates in the Perche region of northern France. Typically grey or black in color, Percherons have a reputation for their intelligence and innate willingness to work.

Ce qui distingue le Percheron des autres chevaux, c'est sa prestance et son style ainsi que sa musculature de cheval de trait. Massif, il peut atteindre plus de 900 kilos, mais sa nature imposante ne fait pas ombrage à son caractère docile. On retrace les origines du cheval dans le Perche, une région du nord de la France. Habituellement de couleur grise ou noire, le Percheron est reconnu pour son sens inné du travail et son intelligence.

El Percherón es reconocido por su elegancia, su estilo y su poderosa musculatura de caballo de tiro. Su peso puede llegar a más de 900 kilos, pero su figura imponente contrasta sutilmente con su docilidad. Raza originaria de la región del Perche, en el norte de Francia, es por lo general de capa gris o negra. El Percherón es reconocido por su inteligencia y su voluntad innata para el trabajo.

QUARTER HORSE / QUARTER HORSE / CUARTO DE MILLA

Blazing fast over short distances, American Quarter Horses have been clocked at speeds up to 55 mph (88.5 km/h) in races of a quarter mile or less. Known for their versatility, good temperament, and "cow sense," Quarter Horses are the most popular breed in the world, with more than four million horses registered. Compact, heavily muscled, and intelligent, this versatile horse is synonymous with Western riding.

Spécialiste de la vitesse, le Quarter Horse peut atteindre près de 90 km/h sur de courtes distances. Caractérisée par sa polyvalence, son caractère agréable et son aptitude pour le travail avec le bétail, cette race est la plus populaire du monde : 4 millions de têtes sont recensées. Compact, musclé et intelligent, le Quarter Horse, polyvalent, est le symbole de l'équitation Western.

De gran rapidez en distancias cortas, el Cuarto de Milla americano ha registrado velocidades de casi 90 km/h en carreras de cuarto de milla (402 metros) o menos. Conocido por su polivalencia, su buen temperamento y su disposición para trabajar con las vacas, el Cuarto de Milla es la raza más popular del mundo, pues cuenta con más de cuatro millones de caballos registrados. Compacto, muy musculoso e inteligente, este caballo polifacético es el símbolo de la monta del Oeste.

SPANISH PUREBRED (P.R.E.) / PURE RACE ESPAGNOLE / PURA RAZA ESPAÑOLA

Linked to the history and culture of Andalusia, the billowing mane, charisma, and unmistakable beauty of the Pura Raza Española, or Pure Spanish Horse, is the calling card for a breed dating back as far as 4,000 B.C. War horse of the Romans, the P.R.E.'s agile, fluid movement gained them popularity among European courts and equestrian academies from the 15th to 18th centuries. The Spanish closed their studbooks to Portugal in 1912, choosing the name P.R.E. instead of "Andalusian."

L'histoire de ce cheval est étroitement liée à la culture andalouse. Les origines de ce cheval à la crinière ondulée, au charisme et à la beauté notoires, remontent à plus de 4 000 ans avant notre ère. Cheval de guerre des Romains, le P.R.E. gagne en popularité avec son agilité et la souplesse de ses mouvements dans les cours d'Europe et les académies équestres du Vieux Continent à partir du 15e siècle, et ce, jusqu'au 18e siècle. Les Espagnols ferment leurs registres d'élevage au Portugal en 1912, choisissant de nommer la race P.R.E. plutôt qu'Andalou.

Vinculado con la historia y la cultura de Andalucía, el caballo de Pura Raza Española es reconocido por su melena ondulante, su carisma y su inconfundible belleza. El origen de esta raza se remonta hasta 4 000 años antes de Cristo. Caballo de guerra de los romanos, el Pura Raza Española gana popularidad en las cortes europeas y las academias ecuestres a partir del siglo XV hasta el XVIII por sus movimientos ágiles y fluidos. En 1912, los españoles cerraron los libros genealógicos a los caballos portugueses y cambiaron el nombre de "caballo andaluz" por Pura Raza Española.

THOROUGHBRED / THOROUGHBRED / PURASANGRE INGLÉS

Consummate racehorses, Thoroughbreds are refined, elegant, sensitive, courageous horses with great stamina. Physically, they have a deep girth area for better breathing, powerful quarters, and strong legs, and stand 16 to 16.2 hands tall on average. Their typical colors are brown, bay or chestnut. Every Thoroughbred traces its ancestry to three foundation stallions imported to England: the Byerley Turk (1689), the Darley Arabian (1705), and the Godolphin Arabian (1728). Many countries have developed their own stamp of Thoroughbred. For example, the Irish Thoroughbred excels in three-day eventing, while the U.S. version is bred for speed and precociousness.

Cheval de course par excellence, le pur-sang est raffiné, élégant, sensible et courageux. Il possède une remarquable endurance, une large circonférence de sanglage pour une meilleure respiration, un derrière puissant et des jambes fortes. Il mesure en moyenne de 16 à 16,2 mains et est habituellement brun, bai ou alezan. Tous les pur-sang sont originalement issus de trois étalons importés de l'Angleterre : Byerley Turk (1689), Darley Arabian (1705) et Godolphin Arabian (1728). De nombreux pays ont produit leur propre signature de pur-sang. Par exemple, le pur-sang irlandais excelle dans les événements s'étalant sur trois jours. La variante américaine est reproduite pour la vitesse et la précocité.

Caballo de carrera de gran talento, el Purasangre Inglés es refinado, elegante, sensible y valiente. Tiene una gran energía, una área de cincha profunda (lo que le permite respirar mejor), cuartos poderosos y patas fuertes. Un purasangre típico mide 16 palmos de altura, y puede ser de pelaje castaño, alazán o café. Todos los caballos Purasangre Inglés modernos son descendientes de alguno de los tres sementales importados a Inglaterra: el Byerley Turk (1689), el Darley Arabian (1705) y el Godolphin Arabian (1728). Muchos países han desarrollado un tipo de purasangre con rasgos particulares; por ejemplo, el de Irlanda se distingue en concursos completos y la versión de Estados Unidos se cría por su velocidad y su precocidad.

WARLANDER / WARLANDER / WARLANDER

The Warlander is a horse of Baroque type that was developed in the 16th century but officially became a breed in 1990 in Australia, by crossing the Iberian horse breed such as the Andalusian and Lusitano with the Friesian breed. Bred for their athletic ability, intelligence, grace and beauty, they are a multi-talented horse that is commonly used

in Show jumping. The Warlander ranges from 14.3 hands high to 16.2 hands high with a coat that can range in any colour. Their calm and willing temperament makes them an all-round great riding horse.

Le warlander est un cheval de type baroque développé au cours du 16e siècle (mais devenu officiellement une race en 1990 en Australie) en croisant un cheval ibérique, comme le pure race espagnole ou le lusitanien, avec le frison. Élevé pour ses qualités athlétiques, son intelligence, sa grâce et sa beauté, c'est un cheval aux multiples talents couramment utilisé pour l'équitation, le dressage, le dressage western, l'endurance et le saut d'obstacles. Le warlander mesure entre 14,3 et 16,2 mains de hauteur et sa robe peut être de n'importe quelle couleur. Son tempérament calme et disposé en fait généralement un bon cheval de selle.

El Warlander es un caballo de tipo barroco desarrollado en el siglo XVI, pero que se consideró oficialmente como una raza en 1990, en Australia. Se trata de una cruza de razas de caballos ibéricos como el Andaluz y el Lusitano con el Frisón. Criado por su capacidad atlética, inteligencia, gracia y belleza, este caballo tiene múltiples talentos y sirve generalmente para el enganche, la doma, la rienda al estilo del Oeste, el enduro y el salto ecuestres. Los Warlanders miden de 14.3 a 16.2 palmos de alzada y tienen capas en cualquier color. Su calma y su buena disposición son características ideales para cualquier tipo de monta.

CANADIAN WARMBLOOD / CANADIAN WARMBLOOD / CANADIENSE DE SANGRE CALIENTE

Consummate racehorses, Thoroughbreds are refined, elegant, sensitive, courageous horses with great stamina. Physically, they have a deep girth area for better breathing, powerful quarters, and strong legs, and stand 16 to 16.2 hands tall on average. Their typical colors are brown, bay or chestnut. Every Thoroughbred traces its ancestry to three foundation stallions imported to England: the Byerley Turk (1689), the Darley Arabian (1705), and the Godolphin Arabian (1728). Many countries have developed their own stamp of Thoroughbred. For example, the Irish Thoroughbred excels in three-day eventing, while the U.S. version is bred for speed and precociousness.

Cheval de course par excellence, le pur-sang est raffiné, élégant, sensible et courageux. Il possède une remarquable endurance, une large circonférence de sanglage pour une meilleure respiration, un derrière puissant et des jambes fortes. Il mesure en moyenne de 16 à 16,2 mains et est habituellement brun, bai ou alezan. Tous les pur-sang sont originalement issus

de trois étalons importés de l'Angleterre : Byerley Turk (1689), Darley Arabian (1705) et Godolphin Arabian (1728). De nombreux pays ont produit leur propre signature de pur-sang. Par exemple, le pur-sang irlandais excelle dans les événements s'étalant sur trois jours. La variante américaine est reproduite pour la vitesse et la précocité.

Caballo de carrera de gran talento, el Purasangre Inglés es refinado, elegante, sensible y valiente. Tiene una gran energía, una área de cincha profunda (lo que le permite respirar mejor), cuartos poderosos y patas fuertes. Un purasangre típico mide 16 palmos de altura, y puede ser de pelaje castaño, alazán o café. Todos los caballos Purasangre Inglés modernos son descendientes de alguno de los tres sementales importados a Inglaterra: el Byerley Turk (1689), el Darley Arabian (1705) y el Godolphin Arabian (1728). Muchos países han desarrollado un tipo de purasangre con rasgos particulares; por ejemplo, el de Irlanda se distingue en concursos completos y la versión de Estados Unidos se cría por su velocidad y su precocidad.

DUTCH WARMBLOOD / HOLLANDAIS À SANG CHAUD (KWPN) / HOLANDÉS DE SANGRE CALIENTE

The Dutch Warmblood is a modern breed, which was first bred in the Netherlands in the 1960's due to the demand for sporting horses. The Dutch Warmblood ranges from 16 hands high to 17 hands high and is usually any solid colour. The Dutch

Warmblood is a quality horse with a great temperament and is capable of most equestrian sports including Show Jumping, Dressage and Eventing. The Dutch Warmblood has become one of the most successful Warmbloods in the world.

Le KWPN est une race moderne reproduite pour la première fois aux Pays-Bas dans les années 1960 en réponse à une demande pour les chevaux sportifs. Il mesure entre 16 et 17 mains de hauteur et est habituellement de couleur unie. Le Hollandais à sang chaud est un cheval de qualité doté d'un bon tempérament et habile dans la plupart des sports équestres incluant le saut d'obstacles, le dressage et le concours complet. Le KWPN est devenu un des chevaux à sang chaud les plus performants dans le monde.

El Holandés de sangre caliente es una raza moderna que se crió por primera vez en los Países Bajos en los años sesenta para satisfacer la demanda de caballos de competición. Estos caballos tienen entre 16 y 17 palmos de alzada y presentan normalmente una capa en cualquier color sólido. El Holandés de sangre caliente es un caballo de calidad con un magnífico temperamento, capaz de competir en la mayor parte de los deportes ecuestres, incluyendo el salto, la doma y el concurso completo. Hoy en día, el Holandés de sangre caliente es uno de los sangre caliente más exitosos del mundo.

Creators

To bring this spectacular production to life, Artistic Director and Creator Normand Latourelle has surrounded himself with some of the brightest creative minds from Quebec and around the world. They have pooled their respective talents to produce the astonishing adventure that is Odysseo.

Les créateurs

Pour donner vie à cette production spectaculaire, le créateur et directeur artistique Normand Latourelle s'est entouré de quelques-uns des esprits les plus créatifs du Québec et d'ailleurs. Ils ont uni leurs talents pour concevoir cette aventure incroyable qu'est *Odysseo*.

Creadores

Para hacer realidad esta espectacular producción, el director artístico y creador Normand Latourelle se ha rodeado de algunas de las más brillantes mentes creativas de Quebec y de otras regiones del mundo. Han unido sus talentos para producir la asombrosa aventura que es *Odysseo*.

Normand Latourelle
Creator and Artistic Director
Créateur et directeur artistique
Creador y Director artístico

Wayne Fowkes
Director and Choreographer
Chorégraphe et Metteur en scène
Director y coreógrapho

Michel Cusson
Composer
Compositeur
Compositor

Guillaume Lord
Set designer
Scénographe
Decorados

Michèle Hamel
Costume Designer
Conceptrice des costumes
Diseñador de vestuario

Alain Lortie
Lighting Designer
Concepteur des éclairages
Diseñador de iluminación

Geodezik – Étienne Cantin
Visual Design
Concepteur visuel
Diseñador visual

Geodezik – Gabriel Coutu-Dumont
Visual Design
Concepteur visuel
Diseñador visual

Geodezik – Olivier Goulet
Visual Design
Concepteur visuel
Diseñador visual

Darren Charles
Dance Choreographer
Chorégraphe de danse
Coreógrafo de danza

Alain Gauthier
Choreographer for The Angels scene
Chorégraphe du numéro Les Anges
Coreógrafo del Número "The Angels"

Elsie Morin
Les Oiseaux du Paradis
Choreographer for Carosello scene
and design of the rotating poles
Chorégraphe du numéro Carosello
et conceptrice des mâts rotatifs
Coreógrafo del Número "Carosello"
y diseñador de "mástiles rotativos

Mathieu Roy
Les Oiseaux du Paradis
Choreographer for Carosello scene
and design of the rotating poles
Chorégraphe du numéro Carosello
et concepteur des mâts rotatifs
Coreógrafo del Número "Carosello"
y diseñador de "mástiles rotativos

Louis Bond
Hair Stylist
Coiffures
Cabello

Georges Lévesque

Every member of the Odysseo team keeps close to their heart their exchanges with the inimitably talented, creative costume designer, Georges Lévesque. Georges passed away mere days before the premiere of Odysseo in Montreal.

Tous les membres de l'équipe d'Odysseo conservent dans leur cœur leur relation avec le créateur de costumes à l'imagination féconde et au talent inimitable, Georges Lévesque. Georges est décédé quelques jours avant la première d'Odysseo à Montréal.

Cada miembro del equipo Odysseo mantiene cerca de su corazón los intercambios y tratos con el inimitable talento creativo del diseñador de vestuario Georges Lévesque. Georges murió pocos días antes del estreno de Odysseo en Montreal.

The Artists

The Cavalia troupe is based in Quebec, Canada, and features acrobats, aerialists, dancers and riders from a number of countries around the world, including the United States, Canada, Brazil, France, Guinea (Africa), Poland, Russia, Spain, Ukraine, South Africa, and Italy. Together, our two-legged performers and our equine stars will take you on an unforgettable journey of discovery.

Les artistes

Établie au Québec (Canada), la troupe de Cavalia regroupe des acrobates, des aériens, des danseurs et des cavaliers d'une quantité de pays, dont le Canada, les États-Unis, le Brésil, la France, la Guinée, la Pologne, la Russie, l'Espagne, l'Ukraine, l'Afrique du Sud et l'Italie. Ensemble, nos artistes bipèdes et nos vedettes quadrupèdes vous feront vivre une expérience de découverte mémorable.

Los artistas

Establecida en Quebec, Canadá, la compañía Cavalia cuenta en su seno con acróbatas, artistas aéreos, bailarines y jinetes de varios países: Canadá, Estados Unidos, Brasil, Francia, Guinea, Polonia, Rusia, España, Ucrania, Africa del Sura e Italia. Juntos, los artistas y las estrellas equinas lo harán vivir un inolvidable viaje de descubrimiento.

 Lucas Altemeyer

 Éric Auclair

 Mathieu Bianchi

 Éric Boudreault

 Ludivine Brousseau

 Maelle Devreton

 Benoit Drouet

 Romain Drouet

 Guillaume Dubrana

 Lucas Eduardo

 Nicolo Francis Kehrwald

 Charles Lamarche

 Yoann Levesque

 Karolina Melska

 Élodie Nonis

 Pavel Skyba

 Ibrahima Sory Socko

 Valentina Spreca

 Gabriel Suski

 Ibrahima Sory Sylla

Alseny Camara

Mamady Camara

Névine Chouraqui

Sacha Giordani Colantoni

Amara Conde

Adrien Crespo-Delbaere

Mohamed Conte

Serge Gamache

Jonatan Gil Delgado

Monize Gmach

Jeremy Gutierrez

SaiLen Jaeger

Chelsea Jordan

Camille Kaczmarek

Maksym Ovchynnikov

Julissa Panus

Elisa Penello

Louis-Pier Racicot

Estelle Sartori

Anton Savytskyi

Anouck Sirvent

Batraz Tsokolaev

Elise Verdoncq

Jacqueline Ward
Kehrwald

Credits / Crédits / Los Créditos

MUSICIANS / MUSICIENS / MÚSICOS

ÉRIC AUCLAIR
ÉRIC BOUDREAULT
SERGE GAMACHE
LOUIS-PIER RACICOT
VALENTINA SPRECA

ARTISTIC / ARTISTIQUE / PERSONAL ARTÍSTICO

SAMUEL ALVAREZ
Resident Artistic Director
Directeur artistique résident
Director artístico residente

ANNICK GOUAILLIER
General stage manager
Régisseure générale
Jefa de escena

KALI PRIEUR
Backstage Manager
Régisseure de plateau
Jefa de plató

MATHIEU BIANCHI
Equestrian Director
Directeur équestre
Director ecuestre

BENOIT DROUET
Trainer
Entraîneur
Entrenador

KEITH DUPONT
Trainer
Entraîneur
Entrenador

KILAN BIANCHI
Equestrian Trainer
Entraîneur équestre
Entrenador ecuestre

JUDITH GOBBELS
Equestrian Backstage Manager
Régisseuse des coulisses équestres
Responsable de bastidores ecuestres

JOANIE PÉPIN
Artistic Therapist
Thérapeute artistique
Terapeuta artística

CATHERINE MIREAULT
Head of Wardrobe
Chef costumière
Jefa del vestuario

KANDY KEIRN SCHWANDT
Wardrobe
Costumière
Vestuario

NICOLE RAMIREZ
Wardrobe
Costumière
Vestuario

SONIA WEBER
Wardrobe
Costumière
Vestuario

TICKETING / BILLETTERIE / TAQUILLA

CHANTAL ST-CYR
Box Office Director and
Promotions Manager
Directrice de la billetterie et
chef des promotions
Directora de la taquilla y
Jefe de promociones

JORDAN RUIZ
Box Office Coordinator
Coordonnateur de la billetterie
Coordinador de la taquilla

KYM MERCILLE
Box Office Manager
Gérante de la billetterie
Gerenta de la taquilla

ROMAIN GRONDIN
Box Office Supervisor
Superviseur de la billetterie
Supervisor de la taquilla

NICOLAS TOUTANT
Call Center Supervisor
Superviseur du centre d'appels
Supervisora del centro de llamadas

ALVARO RODRIGUEZ
Call Center Supervisor
Superviseur du centre d'appels
Supervisora del centro de llamadas

XAVIER SERRA-WAGNEUR
Call Center Supervisor
Superviseure du centre d'appels
Supervisora del centro de llamadas

INTI SALINAS
Call Center Supervisor
Superviseure du centre d'appels
Supervisora del centro de llamadas

PHILIPPE LAVOIE
Call Center Supervisor
Superviseur du centre d'appels
Supervisor del centro de llamadas

JADE GAUTHIER-BOUTIN
Call Center Supervisor
Superviseure du centre d'appels
Supervisora del centro de llamadas

TECHNICAL / TECHNIQUE / PERSONAL TÉCNICO

ALEXANDRE FILION
Technical Director
Directeur technique
Director Técnico

JANELLE LEVESQUE
Technical Coordinator
Coordonnatrice technique
Coordinadora Técnico

CHARLES DAVID DOWD
Head Rigger
Chef gréeur
Jefe aparejador

JOSHUA MARRIN
Rigger
Gréeur
Aparejador

FRÉDÉRIC ROUSSEAU
Head of Automation
Chef de l'automation
Jefa de automatización

MARIE-ÈVE GIRARD
Lead Show Carpenter
Charpentier principal de tournée
Carpintera principal de giras

CHARLES DALLAIRE-SIMPSON
Carpenter
Charpentier
Carpintero

MEGAN BACHANT
Carpenter
Charpentière
Carpintero

SYLVAIN GAGNON
Head of Audio
Chef sonorisateur
Jefe de audio

VINCENT NERON
Sound Assistant
Assistant au son
Asistente de sonido

IAN MORTON
Head of Lighting on tour
Chef de l'éclairage en tournée
Jefe de iluminación de gira

FELIX BEZEAU-TREMBLAY
Head of Video / Projections
Chef de la vidéo / projections
Jefe de video y proyecciones

ÉRIC LANDRY
Lighting and Video Operator
Opérateur lumière et vidéo
Operador de iluminación y video

STABLES / ÉCURIES / ESTABLOS

NICOLAS VANDERPLAS
Stables Director
Directeur des écuries
Director de establos

LUC TESSIER
Logistics Coordinator
Coordonnateur de la logistique
Coordinador logístico

MARJOLAINE CAMILLE
Veterinarian Technician
Technicienne vétérinaire
Técnica veterinaria

EMMANUEL FERNANDEZ
Groom
Palefrenier
Mozo de cuadra

EDUARDO VOLLRATH
Groom
Palefrenier
Mozo de cuadra

ALEXE ROUSSEAU
Groom
Palefrenière
Moza de cuadra

ANDRÉANNE DUMONT
Groom
Palefrenière
Moza de cuadra

DAVID VALOIS
Groom
Palefrenier
Mozo de cuadra

NYCKEIJA CHILKO MOON RIDINGTON
Groom
Palefrenière
Moza de cuadra

GABRIELLA CLAVEAU
Groom
Palefrenière
Moza de cuadra

MATHIEU DURANDET
Groom
Palefrenier
Mozo de cuadra

LOGISTICS / LOGISTIQUE / LOGÍSTICA

AURÉLIE VOZAK
Logistics Director
Directrice de la logistique
Directora de la logística

SEAN WARREN
Site Manager
Gérant de site
Gerente de sitio

FERDINANDO ANCESCHI
Tent Master
Chef monteur de tente
Maestro de carpa

MURRAY WRIGHT
Tent Technician
Technicien, monteur de tente
Técnico de carpa

PAULETTE LÉVESQUE
Logistics Assistant
Assistante à la logistique
Asistente de logística

STEVE HALEY
Head Electrician
Chef électricien
Jefe electricista

CHRISTOPHER GOWER
Site Electrician
Électricien de site
Electricista de sitio

BRUNO DAIGLE-GUÉRETTE
Site Technician
Technicien de site
Técnico de sitio

MICHEL HÉBERT
Plumber
Plombier
Plomero

FREDERICK COOKE
Site Technician
Technicien de site
Técnico de sitio

PUBLIC SERVICES / SERVICES AU PUBLIC / SERVICIOS PÚBLICOS

VERONICA HESS
Public services Director
Directrice des services au public
Directora de servicios públicos

TRAVIS PATERSON
Rendez-Vous VIP Tent Supervisor
Superviseur de la tente Rendez-Vous VIP
Supervisor de la carpa Rendez-Vous VIP

CARMEN MURILLO
Food Concessions Supervisor
Superviseue des concessions
alimentaires
Supervisora de puestos de comida

GINA GARCIA
Head Usher
Chef placière
Jefa de acomodadores

ROSIE JANE FRANCIS
Boutique Supervisor
Superviseure de la boutique
Supervisora de la tienda

CHRISTINE TRÉPANIER
VIP Boutique Supervisor
Superviseure de la Boutique VIP
Supervisora de la tienda VIP

SEAN HENNING
Inventory Supervisor
Superviseur de l'inventaire
Supervisor de inventarios

SIMON NUGENT-LÉTOURNEAU
Program Seller
Vendeur de programmes
Vendedor de programas

SERVICES / SERVICES DE TOURNÉE / SERVICIOS DE GIRA

MAXIMILIANA MESINA
Tour Services Director
Directrice des services de tournée
Directora de servicios de gira

SABRINA DANOË BALMIR
Tour Services - Human Resources
Services de tournée – ressources
humaines
Servicios de gira – Recursos humanos

MARY-ÈVE MARTEL
Tour Services Coordinator
Coordonnatrice des services
de tournée
Coordinadora de servicios de gira

MAGALI JAY-SNYDER
Tour Services Coordinator
Coordonnatrice des services
de tournée
Coordinadora de servicios de gira

HERMINIO NEO ALONSO
IT Technician
Technicien des TI
Técnico de TI

JOSE LUIS ACEVEDO CHAVEZ
Executive Chef
Chef cuisinier
Jefe de cocina

MARIE-EVE JOMPHE
Sous Chef
Sous-chef
Segundo de cocina

JAMES FRANCIS
Sous Chef
Sous-chef
Segundo de cocina

CARRIE SHEPPARD
Sous Chef - VIP
Sous-chef - VIP
Segundo de cocina - VIP

SOUVENIR PROGRAM / PROGRAMME SOUVENIR / PROGRAMA OFICIAL

JO-ANNE MARTIN
Project Manager
Directrice de projets
Directora de proyectos

OLIVIER MÉNARD
Graphic Designer
Graphiste
Diseñador gráfico

LOUISE MEILLEUR
Consultant / Consultante / Consultora

SHONDA SECORD
Texts / Textes / Textos

PHOTOGRAPHERS / PHOTOGRAPHES / FOTÓGRAFOS

FRANÇOIS BERGERON
JEAN-FRANÇOIS LEBLANC
PASCAL RATTHÉ
SHELLEY PAULSON
ALEXANDRE LEGAULT-DÉRY
SOPHIE LAUGHREA
CHRIS WAITS

MURAH	ARABIAN / ARABE / ÁRABE
NDALUZ	LUSITANO / LUSITANIEN / LUSITANO
RTISTRY	ARABIAN / ARABE / ÁRABE
AILEY	APPALOOSA / APPALOOSA / APPALOOSA
ELLO	SPANISH PURE BRED / PURE RACE ESPAGNOLE/ PURA RAZA ESPAÑOLA
OMBAY	SPANISH PURE BRED / PURE RACE ESPAGNOLE/ PURA RAZA ESPAÑOLA
RAVAS	HALF-ARABIAN / DEMI SANG ARABE / MITAS ÁRABE
HIEF	ARABIAN / ARABE / ÁRABE
ODY	APPALOOSA / APPALOOSA / APPALOOSA
OUMBA	QUARTER HORSE / QUARTER HORSE / CUARTO DE MILLA
OWBOY	QUARTER HORSE / QUARTER HORSE / CUARTO DE MILLA
IAMANTE	LUSITANO / LUSITANIEN / LUSITANO
ON MEASTRO	PERCHERON-HANOVERIAN / PERCHERON-HANOVRIEN / PERCHERÓN-HANNOVERIANO
UDE	PAINT HORSE/PAINT HORSE/PAINT HORSE
UNE	WARLANDER/ WARLANDER/ WARLANDER
DITION	ARABIAN / ARABE / ÁRABE
DGE FIELD	DUTCH WARMBLOOD / HOLLANDAIS À SANG CHAUD (KWPN) / HOLANDÉS DE SANGRE CALIENTE
FENDI	ARABIAN / ARABE / ÁRABE
LECTO	LUSITANO / LUSITANIEN / LUSITANO
MBAIXADOR	LUSITANO / LUSITANIEN / LUSITANO
QUADOR	LUSITANO / LUSITANIEN / LUSITANO
-VOGUE	LUSITANO / LUSITANIEN / LUSITANO
ADISTA	LUSITANO / LUSITANIEN / LUSITANO
AROL	SPANISH PURE BRED / PURE RACE ESPAGNOLE/ PURA RAZA ESPAÑOLA
LAUTISTA	LUSITANO / LUSITANIEN / LUSITANO
ROSTY	ARABIAN / ARABE / ÁRABE
URIOSO	LUSITANO / LUSITANIEN / LUSITANO
ALENO	LUSITANO / LUSITANIEN / LUSITANO
AVILAN	SPANISH PURE BRED / PURE RACE ESPAGNOLE/ PURA RAZA ESPAÑOLA
EE GEE	ARABIAN / ARABE / ÁRABE
RECO	SPANISH PURE BRED / PURE RACE ESPAGNOLE/ PURA RAZA ESPAÑOLA
UADALEVIN	SPANISH PURE BRED / PURE RACE ESPAGNOLE/ PURA RAZA ESPAÑOLA
US	ARABIAN / ARABE / ÁRABE
ERITAGE	ARABIAN / ARABE / ÁRABE
URACAN	SPANISH PURE BRED / PURE RACE ESPAGNOLE/ PURA RAZA ESPAÑOLA
NDIO	LUSITANO / LUSITANIEN / LUSITANO
NTREPIDO	SPANISH PURE BRED / PURE RACE ESPAGNOLE/ PURA RAZA ESPAÑOLA
ACKSON	QUARTER HORSE / QUARTER HORSE / CUARTO DE MILLA
UGLANS	SPANISH PURE BRED / PURE RACE ESPAGNOLE/ PURA RAZA ESPAÑOLA
UGUETON	SPANISH PURE BRED / PURE RACE ESPAGNOLE/ PURA RAZA ESPAÑOLA
ODA	APPALOOSA / APPALOOSA / APPALOOSA
AWSON	THOUROUGHBRED-QUARTER HORSE / PUR SANG-QUARTER HORSE / PURA RAZA - CUARTO DE MILLA
EMONCELLO	CANADIAN WARMBLOOD / CANADIAN WARMBLOOD / CANADIENSE DE SANGRE CALIENTE
IMENO	SPANISH PURE BRED / PURE RACE ESPAGNOLE/ PURA RAZA ESPAÑOLA
MELCHOR	SPANISH PURE BRED / PURE RACE ESPAGNOLE/ PURA RAZA ESPAÑOLA
MIKKO	PAINT HORSE / PAINT HORSE / PAINT HORSE
MOOSE	QUARTER HORSE / QUARTER HORSE / CUARTO DE MILLA
MOTION	ARABIAN / ARABE / ÁRABE
AZARENO	LUSITANO / LUSITANIEN / LUSITANO
EZMA	ARABIAN / ARABE / ÁRABE
MERIO	LUSITANO / LUSITANIEN / LUSITANO
EARL	ARABIAN / ARABE / ÁRABE
INSAPO	SPANISH PURE BRED / PURE RACE ESPAGNOLE/ PURA RAZA ESPAÑOLA
UNTO	SPANISH PURE BRED / PURE RACE ESPAGNOLE/ PURA RAZA ESPAÑOLA
QUARTZ	FRENCH SADDLE HORSE / CHEVAL DE SELLE FRANÇAIS / SILLA FRANCÉS
EDINO	SPANISH PURE BRED / PURE RACE ESPAGNOLE/ PURA RAZA ESPAÑOLA
ANJAR	ARABIAN / ARABE / ÁRABE
HANGRI LA	ARABIAN / ARABE / ÁRABE
HMITTY	QUARTER HORSE / QUARTER HORSE / CUARTO DE MILLA
HAKE	ARABIAN / ARABE / ÁRABE
ILVER	ARABIAN / ARABE / ÁRABE
OLDIER BOY	DUTCH WARMBLOOD / HOLLANDAIS À SANG CHAUD (KWPN) / HOLANDÉS DE SANGRE CALIENTE
UTOR ARENAS	SPANISH PURE BRED / PURE RACE ESPAGNOLE/ PURA RAZA ESPAÑOLA
TAH	PAINT HORSE / PAINT HORSE / PAINT HORSE
ATARA	CANADIAN HORSE / CANADIEN / CABALLO CANADIENSE
URICH	CANADIAN HORSE / CANADIEN / CABALLO CANADIENSE